A Super Duper Book Brand

Written by
Mercy B Carruthers

TABLE OF **CONTENTS**

Introduction

As an African American storyteller, I've learned that the methods others use for branding and the promotion of their books are far more different than those of my community. Our audience has an entirely different perception of the art of reading and speak a totally different language when it comes to the topic and/or task.

There was a time when I studied branding from *YouTube* and other literary resources that I thought would enhance my brand only to discover those tactics simply didn't work for me. This isn't a one size fits all type of deal. African American storytellers cater to a unique audience and I felt that it was time to package my knowledge into a series of books that are dedicated to educating storytellers like myself.

A Super Duper Book Brand

Written by
Mercy B Carruthers

Chapter One

The Basis of Branding

The misconception that branding is a logo, a color scheme, a slogan, or a website homepage tends to linger when one is faced with the question of branding. Yes, these elements are detrimental to branding, but does not define the word itself. In fact, branding is much more simple than one would imagine.

Branding is the perception others have of you. It is what identifies you. Branding is the beauty of recognition beyond physical aspects of your business and/or persona. Branding is the thought that others have when hearing your name or the name of your business. Branding is a direct representation of you, what you stand for, and what you do.

So often I see people scrambling to purchase different products to 'start' branding, when in truth, the best form of branding is costless. The best way to build a reputable brand is by being present, being consistent, being authentic, being valuable, and becoming unforgettable. As an author, these aspects of your brand happen to be free, not costing you a red cent.

I began building my brand over three years ago, which was before I published my first book. Now, years later, I have built a sustainable brand through vigorous methods that I want to share with authors such as myself to ease the road to greatness. Branding isn't the easiest task, but it is well worth the hassle.

➤ How is branding important for authors?

Branding is essential for any entrepreneur, which happens to be the hat authors decide to wear when entering the literary realm. There isn't a business that I've seen prosper with horrible branding. There is a plethora of reasons branding is important for authors, which I will began listing:

1. Branding is especially essential to African American authors because it is highly beneficial to your career and offers incredible value to your writing and overall persona.

2. Branding helps differentiate you from other authors who are in the same industry as you, and possibly write similar books as you.
3. Branding gives a better perception of your work, your core values, and adds countless attributes to your proceedings as an author.
4. Branding increases your visibility.
5. Branding creates a foundation.
6. Branding helps you attract new and potential readers.
7. Branding helps you build a loyal fan base.
8. Branding helps you build quality relationships.
9. Branding builds trust amongst your audience.
10. Branding creates an impenetrable layer of authenticity.
11. Branding converts potential readers into books purchased and pages read.
12. Branding helps you snag speaking opportunities and creates influence amongst others.

➢ How does good branding look?

The question should be, 'How does good branding sound?'

The physical attributes of a brand are only bonuses.

A good brand sounds like:
- Target
- Walmart
- Ikea
- Chipotle
- Krispy Kreme
- Marvel Studios
- Dr. Seuss
- Bishop T.D. Jakes
- Will Smith
- Beyoncé
- Nicki Minaj
- Drake
- Oprah Winfrey
- Shonda Rhimes
- Kerry Washington
- Tyler Perry

These are only a few examples of how good branding sound. Before you moved on to the next business or name, I'm certain you took a quick second to allow an image, word or thought to confirm the identity of each subject listed. This didn't happen voluntarily, but these brands are so well-built that your mind wandered without warning.

There are no pictures insight, but you're aware of what these business or people represent or stand for. You're also immediately equipped with the knowledge of their values and what makes them so memorable. That is how good branding sounds! At all times, this is the reaction you should strive to receive from readers across the globe.

When readers hear the name, Mercy B Carruthers, I don't want them to have to second guess or question, "What does she write?" I want it to be an afterthought, with the first thing coming to mind is that I write amazing, emotion-provoking and stereotypical-defying stories about black love that harbors male characters that make you want to throw away your real-life boo for a book bae. That is my aim. That is what I want my brand to sound like.

➢ **What does branding mean for authors?**

Branding for authors means creating something dynamic enough to be remembered by your audience. Yes, we're in a space where covers resemble, stock models are reused, titles collide, typography on covers all look the same, and we all have black stories bursting through our pages. However, this doesn't mean that you must keep swimming in the direction of the school of fish. Branding is taking the initiative to swim on the side of the school of fish or even go your own route.

Branding means stepping up and standing out. It means a world of a difference. There are so many authors that I see who can write really well and have amazing stories that are being told, but they are drowning in the sea of authors. They're being looked over and passed up for stories that are potentially a bit less intriguing and interesting than theirs.

You want to know why?

They've decided that building a brand is too much work, not necessary, or developed a phobia about the topic itself. These authors rarely show up, rarely reach out, and rarely get the recognition that they are due. Branding can mean the difference between flourishing royalties and stressful nights thinking about the lack of growth you're witnessing in your reader base. Please, choose to brand.

➢ **How have you branded yourself as an author?**

I could linger on this question for the duration of the book because I've tried so many tactics, but I will try to keep this short and simple, being that I will dive into my branding experiences later in this book.

1. I became confident in myself and what I had to offer to the world of literature.
2. I read my ass off until I was certain that the types of stories I had to tell would survive in the industry that I wanted to break into.
3. I put my pride aside and wasn't afraid to reach out to people; readers, writers, and potential readers. Whomever.
4. I was sure to get a clear understanding of who I wanted to be in the industry.
5. I didn't deter or shy away from the sight of hard work. Ultimately, I understood that the most highly regarded people of the world didn't come by their successful position by sitting on their asses. They worked.
6. I understood that it was a process and legacies aren't built in a day.

➢ What are some mistakes you see authors making as it pertains to branding?

Considering their brand is a logo, colors, business cards, a certain font, or a nice banner to showcase at events, that is all wrong. Those are simply physical attributes that contribute to identifying you as a brand, but a brand is simple and intangible. It's a thought. It is what you've led people to believe of you and your business.

When I think of *Target*, of course the red circle with the dot in the middle comes to mind, but more importantly, I think of quality and cleanliness. The red circle with the dot means nothing in comparison to the value that I know I'll receive inside of the *Target* stores.

Other mistakes I've witnessed are the lack of branding at all, confusion within branding, personal branding colliding with business branding, and some others that I can't recall from the top of my dome.

The biggest mistake is authors thinking that they don't want 'a brand' or don't need to brand. In my opinion, it's ridiculous to even consider. I can't understand what would possess one to think that not branding is better than branding – other than the lack of knowledge on the topic in general.

Branding gives you a VOICE as an author. You should always consider the task even when it seems harder than you may have anticipated. Truthfully, committing to a few key consistent endeavors will help you brand yourself effectively, without overworking and tiring yourself out.

When it comes to confusion in branding, many authors are simply clueless of where to start, what the word means, or how to create a reputable brand. It is simple, be who you are and be that person openly. Authors who happen to shy away from their craft are the ones who lack the backing they need when it comes to branding. Be bold in your writings and intentions and branding will fall into place. Be visible and generate consistency with content and core values across the board and your brand will develop itself before you know it.

I had a discussion with an author just recently about the final mistake mentioned. Personal and business branding colliding. African American authors (mostly fictional writers who publish through *Amazon*) utilize *Facebook* as a place to generate relationships and build their reader base. I love the idea, but we must be very careful. Social media is used to be social, but when it comes to business, it is used to do business.

If you're attempting to build a 'serious' brand, but every time I get on *Facebook*, I see you posting memes that have nothing to do with your current work in progress or past projects, but of videos with your opinion that is useless and doesn't relate to the content that I read from you, or you are forever complaining about something, then when I hear or see your name, I will not relate it to your writings. Instead, I will probably associate it with the annoyance of your personal life splattered over a *Facebook* page that I befriended in order to keep up with your releases.

It is important to separate the two unless your personal and business brand go hand-in-hand. Some people live the life they write about, so shying away from their personal lives aren't necessary. Personally, I have a *Facebook* page for books and business while also having one for personal usage. As an author, be mindful of what you're posting and how it can affect your brand for better or worse.

TAKEAWAYS

_____
_____
_____
_____
_____
_____
_____
_____
_____
_____
_____
_____
_____
_____
_____
_____
_____
_____
_____

TAKEAWAYS

_____

_____

_____

_____

_____

_____

_____

_____

_____

_____

_____

_____

_____

_____

_____

_____

_____

_____

_____

_____

Chapter Two

Building A Solid Foundation Through Branding

Have you ever purchased a product from a brand that you've never seen, have no knowledge of, or doesn't have the same core values as you? Me either. I happen to call these pop-up brands. They pop-up out of nowhere and expect you to hurry up and buy what they're selling without a clear understanding of who they are and how they can bring value to your life.

Let's take the millions of *Instagram* hair companies that continue to pop-up by the dozens each day. I've gotten tons of direct messages encouraging me to purchase hair at both wholesale and retail price. I always end up deleting the messages and moving forward with my day. I mean, I don't know who these people are and I've never heard of their brand. Why would I spend money with someone when there is possibly no trust involved in the transaction?

People spend their time, money, and energy on brands that they can trust, which is why building that trust is so important. I have friends who have asked me for countless tips on starting businesses. The first thing I tell them is to begin building trust amongst potential customers. It's crazy that they take the advice and shit on it. Literally. Before I know it, I see a website with their domain attached and a flyer of some sort soliciting money from 'potential' customers with whom I specifically advised them to build trust.

It happens every time. And, you want to know what else happens? Their lack of foundation causes their 'business' to fail before it even starts. I've seen it happen countless amounts of times. So, don't be a pop-up author. Don't shit on the advice I'm about to give you as my friends do the advice that I share with them. Utilize every point made in this chapter as your guide to building a foundation through branding.

➤ How can you begin building a foundation through branding?

Foundation (according to *Google*) is defined as an underlying basis or principle for something. Simply stated, level one. Ground zero. It is the basis of which you build from. Without a foundation, your structure is bound to crumble. Foundations are fundamental. They're necessary.

Building a foundation starts with discovering your target audience and how you – as a person – can contour your content to connect with them seamlessly. This does not mean altering who you are, your core values, or your purpose. It is simply the act of determining how to correlate them in a way that resonates with the people you are determined to reach. Basically, you must begin to speak the same language to convey the message.

Again, by no means must you alter your persona. Stay true to who you are and the people that are for you, will find you. Yet, you must convey your message in a way that is able to be comprehended by more than just you or the few people around you. I call it code-switching.

So, to begin, discover your target audience and their language. Become fluent and speak to them often. Don't shy away from conversation. Keep the floor open.

You can do this by:

1. Starting a blog.
2. Starting an email list.
3. Starting a reading group.
4. Starting a *Facebook* business page.
5. Interacting with your future readers through private messaging.

6.   Creating questions targeting your audience on your social media profiles to post.

➢ How do you discover your target audience?

There's ALWAYS someone in mind who you're writing to. Always. When I am writing, there's a slightly blurred profile of the woman I expect to read my books. Because I was an avid reader before I was a writer, I had the pleasure of discovering my target audience before I began writing. It was already set in stone that I would be writing the same types of stories I read, so I knew that the readers I wanted to attract were probably like me.

Knowing what enticed me helped me to figure out what would entice my audience. So, I began researching and trying to understand why these things enticed me and how I could implement them in my brand once I started. I studied my target, night and day, to figure out the activity of their days in order to capture the ideal of what their lives were like and how I could insert myself into them as often as I could.

• Listen to their concerns.

- Understand their cries.
- Be aware of their situations and circumstances.
- Be sociable with them before you even publish your book.
- Find their hideouts and frequent them.
- Become a face in your community (or the one you are building).

➢ Once you know who you are targeting, how do you appeal to them?

Knowing who you're targeting is only a piece of the puzzle. Acting on your knowledge is another portion. Now that you know where your people are, what their interests are, and what their days consist of, you're wondering where to go from there?

Let's make this as simple as possible and take *Instagram* for an example. I follow a lot of my clients. If I absolutely can't figure out what to create to appeal to them, I can simply use the "FOLLOWING" feature under the like tap and browse the content that my clients have been most responsive to. Once I've discovered this content, I understand what is more appealing to and what they gravitate to more. This will lead me to making more relevant content that I'm certain will resonate with them.

If you'd like to try this technique with *Facebook*, take a peek at what they're liking the most. See what they're commenting on. Use this to CREATE but NOT COPY. Do not copy other's content. Cater your content to your audience based on what is more appealing to their eyes.

➢ How do we convince people to trust our brand?

You don't. People must grow to trust your brand on their own and this usually comes from consistency, visibility and repetition. Studies show that one must come into direct contact with a brand on an average of seven times before investing in that brand. Well, if you're always in the shadows, then how will readers see you and know to invest in your brand?

Word of mouth is the best way to create trust within a brand, but you must first gain those readers that will even begin to sing your praises. The authenticity of a brand elevates its trust level. When readers find your brand to be true, they begin to trust it. This declaration is only derived through consistency and repetition. Giving them quality work and reads on a consistent basis, whether every month or every four months, so that they'll have something to look forward to. Show them that they can count on you. Show them that you are reliable.

➤ What makes people follow brands?

- Appeal.
- Perception.
- Authenticity.
- Word of mouth.
- Consistency.
- Relationship building.
- Trust.
- Confidence.

➤ How do I build before I start selling?

Building your foundation is the key to the start of successful selling as an author. As many say, "Come out of the gate swinging." Lay the foundation so that your climb to the top is a bit smoother and the layers on top will be more stable. Here are some ways to begin building before selling:

1. Friend readers. They are not hard to find. If you're a reader, then you all possibly hang in the same hideouts.

2. Announce your desires to enter the literary realm. Gauge a response from potential readers and supporters. Allow them to encourage you while interacting and sharing your fears.

3. Later, announce your actual entry into the literary realm or the start of your new (or first) book. Don't shy away from the conversations made under your posts.

4. Document your writing process.

5. Direct message or private message the readers to introduce yourself and give a little detail about your upcoming project.

6. Share FREE content such as short stories so that readers can get a taste of your writing.

7. Give sneak peeks of your work in progress in order to gauge a reaction and create suspense and anticipation amongst readers.

8. Blog.
9. Share graphics pertaining to your book on your social media outlets.
10. Conduct live readings on your pages.

These tips are helpful in preparing your readers for what is to come and avoid being a "pop-up" author who drops a link and expects the world to click it. Begin building your foundation as soon as you possibly can!

➢ How do I narrow down my audience?

It is important to narrow your client base to better target your audience. The game isn't to try and sell to everyone, but to sell to a specific type of person. Do not generalize your market, specialize and minimize. The more centered and focused your audience is, the more people you can reach. It's okay to target one specific group because this doesn't necessarily mean that others won't flock to your business. It's simply a way of creating better content versus being all over the place.

It is imperative to your success as an author that you know who you are writing for and to. Give your ideal reader a name. When speaking about them, call them by name. This helps you connect with them and resonate with them as you're strategizing to capture their attention and convert them into your audience.

There are specific characteristics that you need to know about your ideal reader in order to write for them and market to them. The list below is all of the aspects of your ideal reader that you should know before you even begin generating content for them.

1. Gender
2. Ethnicity
3. Age range
4. Income bracket
5. Beliefs
6. Values
7. Lifestyle
8. Work hours
9. Student
10. Parents
11. Likes/Dislikes
12. Stature/Looks
13. Background/Childhood
14. Issues
15. Concerns
16. Hobbies/Shows/Sports

Knowing these things will help determine when and how you can be most effective to your audience. When you know them by heart, you cannot lose. Implement these characteristics into your content strategy. You need to know whether your ideal reader will engage with certain aspects. The delivery will be different depending on every aspect listed above. Knowing exactly who you are targeting helps make your content centralized instead of generalized.

For example, are you targeting male or female readers? This helps you create a brand color palette for your content. It is your job to know what your audience prefers. Make sure that when you build your brand that you are appealing to either male or females.

With urban fiction, the reader bases are more black people, so knowing this, you know not to put a bunch of what Becky likes all over your content calendar. You need to find out who you are targeting to before you even begin writing or devising a marketing strategy. People respond differently, and it is your responsibility to figure out what your readers will respond to. But first, you need to know who that reader is.

Young people do not have the same mindset as older people. I don't write for young people. I write for people who have storms they've overcome or are currently in. I write for people who experience things in life. My books are intended to give them an escape from those storms and experiences, so I don't write for people who can't relate. So, when I write, I don't write childlike. My sentences are complex because my audience is complex. They deserve more in-depth.

Get to know who your readers are. One thing I hate for writers to say is, "I'm shy." If you are shy, then writing is not for you. In six months, when no one knows you, how shy will you be? At some point, you have to come out. Readers won't come and find you, it is your job to find them. Come out swinging at your audience members.

Get in your readers' business. I create characters that are based on my readers business. For example, I asked them what would be their ideal mate? A unanimous answer was, "Someone who likes children because I have two." So, I implemented that in my book. My current work had a man with a child who was attracted to a woman. He struggled with whether she would accept his child.

Readers have different feelings when they can relate to characters and situations. When things are directly related to your audience, you have a better chance at connecting and keeping that readers' attention. Write for a specific person and make their dreams come true in your books. Give your readers a voice through your books. In my books, I root for the underdogs. I do this because my readers are the underdogs. No one is rooting for them, no one expects them to win, but I make them win in my books.

Have a visual, whether you draw them or cut them out from a magazine or the internet. Always have that visual presence when you write. It helps you know how to write and exactly what to say that will resonate with the person you are ultimately writing for. As previously stated, you do not write for you, you write for your readers.

Triggers are the things that get your readers going, stir up their emotions, cause them to engage, and bring them out of hiding. It is important to have triggers because triggers create influence, you must first capture one's attention. You can't capture their attention without triggering an interest within them at some point.

You trigger your reader by using the reader analysis above. You've created your target reader already. Use her/his makeup in order to come up with catchy ways to grab hold of your readers' attention.

For example, my strategy includes displaying a profound love for the alpha female that is submissive to only her male counterpart. This spills over into my writing. This means my main female characters suffer from daddy issues, and partners with men of dominance to combat those issues of neglect stemming from their father.

When you stir up emotions, you have their attention. When you can do something, and people don't care, then you don't have them. Find ways to make your readers pay attention. Find ways to make them interested in what you are writing. Find something that they are passionate about and implement that in your writing.

TAKEAWAYS

_____

_____

_____

_____

_____

_____

_____

_____

_____

_____

_____

_____

_____

_____

_____

_____

_____

_____

TAKEAWAYS

_____

_____

_____

_____

_____

_____

_____

_____

_____

_____

_____

_____

_____

_____

_____

_____

_____

_____

_____

_____

Chapter Three

Branding Within Your Books

Just the other day, I was joking with an author friend about how the authors that produce the longest books have the most loyal and largest fan base. They also tend to have the most reviews and support in general. It is ways such as this that writers are able to brand themselves through their writing. Without ever having to say it from their own mouths, readers of authors who write longer novels (one hundred thousand plus words per book), know a few things:

1. They will be thoroughly satisfied for hours on end when they sit to read that particular author's books.
2. It will be months (sometimes a year) before they receive another book from the author, unless the author has a series that he/she completed before releasing book one.
3. The author may be quiet or not present on social media due to their attention being solely on their manuscript.

4.   The story is – more than likely – not rushed and won't end as briefly as other books.

This is representation that you are able to brand within your writing. Yet, this is only one example of authors branding within their writing. There are many ways that you can brand within your books. If you take the time to develop a consistent brand within your writings, it eliminates many of the tasks you'd need to complete in order to brand outside of your books. Authors who brand through their writing have a less difficult time branding themselves through vigorous tasks that are linked through authors who are simply 'just writing'. Don't ever just write, please. Be strategic!

J.K. Rowling.
Sheesh.

Let's take *Harry Potter* for an example. The author has branded herself through a seven-book series that opens a world of fantasy beyond anyone's wildest dreams. Though she has other books, when you think of J.K. Rowling, the first thing that comes to mind is *Harry Potter*. That is branding. Branding through writing.

While Rowling also writes under a different pen name, her most successful series remains *Harry Potter*. The series has taken on a life of its own and became the core of Rowling's brand. I can't even say her name without thinking of flying objects and spells.

E.L. James.
Sheesh.

James penned the *Fifty Shades Trilogy* along with *Darker*, which is Grey's account of everything. When you think of E.L., your first thoughts are possibly the pandemonium that she was able to cause through her series. You may even consider her goals as an author. Otherwise, you'll probably think that she is able to bring out the freak in the dullest of people.

These accusations are simple a part of her brand and ole girl has branded well! Again, I can't say her name without getting a little thud in my undies knowing what goes down in her books. If a book can make me feel that way, please believe that I am willing to support nearly whatever she comes forth with.

Terri Woods.

You know her. We all know her. The first thought that comes to mind is both Gena and Quadir. Also the thought of REAL URBAN FICTION. Whenever I lack the urge to read the genre that helped me with my start, I gravitate to *True to the Game*, which was written by Woods, because according to me, she's notorious for writing classic urban fiction novels.

Steve Harvey

I'm aware of the fact that if I pick up a Steve Harvey book, I'm going to learn a lesson of some sort. Steve has branded himself as an author and a speaker to learn from. If I am in the mood to be taught a lesson, it is a book from Steve that I'll possibly consider.

These are simply examples of how authors are able to brand themselves through their writing. I felt it necessary to give these examples so that you can better understand what I mean when I say that it is possible. Also, so that you won't consider me foolish for believing it.

➤ How can I brand myself through writing?

Pick a niche.
Pick a genre.
Pick a certain type of plot.
Pick a certain type of heroine.
Pick a topic to ALWAYS include in your books.

Pick a moral.
Pick a word count.
Pick a cover scheme.
Pick and choose!

If you're attempting to brand yourself through writing, it is very important that you understand that once you choose one of the options from above, you must stick with it. So, in my opinion, chose one of the options that you can still work around and not confine yourself for future purposes.

As mentioned, Rowling writes under a second pen name. As an author who writes under a second pen name as well, I can almost bet that – although successful – the *Harry Potter* series tied her in a box; meaning that it was detrimental to her sanity and career as a passionate writer to produce under another pen name in order to give her other books a chance of survival. With the *Potter* series, there is a special type of audience, which possibly expects one type of book from her. As a creator, our minds wander. Obviously, that isn't all Rowling wants to write about.

Word Count.

Easy. Writers usually know their limits. Continue to strive for the same – or around the same – count each time that you write and readers will become accustomed to the length of your books and begin to expect this. This style of branding is more logical and easier to bend and break the pattern without backlash or the possibility of losing your readers' interest.

Genre.

It isn't the easiest to follow through, but it is a very potent way to brand yourself through writing. Personally, this is the reason that I have two pen names. I desired writing outside of my chosen genre. Yet, some people prefer staying in one genre and not hopping. If this is your preference, then choose a genre and stick with it. Now, when people need a good book in a certain category, they know to come to you because you never stray.

Type of heroine/hero.

This is an easy one as well. I will take Love Belvin, a prolific storyteller, for example. Love chooses a certain type of hero and heroine to write about in each of her books. As a fictitious therapist, she visualizes her main characters as patients. To write your story, you must have a big enough issue for her to take on your case.

(I hope I'm getting this right. Love, forgive me if I'm misconstruing your words.)

So, in conclusion, Love only takes on clients with crucial issues that need immediate attention. Something is tattered within all of her main characters and you will find her rehabbing them throughout the book.

Type of niche.

Let's go with B.M. Hardin. Personally, I've never read a B.M. Hardin book, BUT that's the good part about this mention. I've never read a book, but when I say her name, something in particular comes to mind. As of lately, she'd been on this wave. Her heroines have been CRAZY. I can see this by the cover and reading the synopsis of her books. I'm not sure how long she's kept this up, but I have recently caught on to the trend of hers.

Trust me, whenever I have the urge to read about a crazy ass woman who's scorn by love, she will be the first person I seek. It isn't only me. Readers pick up on these things and when they're in the mood for the thing that you specialize in, you'll be the first they come to.

➢ Why do you suggest branding through writing?

The whole point of you reading this book is because you want to step up and stand out, right? Well, that is why I suggest branding through writing.

I wouldn't tell you to do something that I wouldn't do myself. I've chosen a few options from above.

Type of heroine.

I can't recall a heroine of mine having a good relationship with her father. All of my heroines have daddy issues. Simply because I know them all too well. I have them, too. These are the women that I can portray best. As well, my heroines are strong and reliable people, who only bend for the man that they grow to love.

Type of hero.

My heroes are irresistible. They make you consider dropping your boo for an imaginary one. They are providers and protectors. They are fearless. They are strong and reek of authority. Yet, they are pudding when it comes to their heroine. I mean, they are a different kind of person when she's in the room.

Type of genre.

Urban fiction. That goes without saying. I write about urban love stories and I love it. There is nothing like showcasing black love.

A moral.

My stories all have the same moral. Black men are capable of loving a woman properly, no matter what the media and the world tells you. As well, black love isn't something to turn away from. It is to be embraced and idolized. Black people have been through so much and to still find love in our hearts is beautiful.

In these choices, I've been able to brand myself and stand out amongst others. Many readers consider my writings classic and I'm appreciative of that. That is the legacy that I want to create for myself. If you want to leave a lasting impression on your readers, then I highly suggest you make your choices as well.

➤ Should I compromise my diversity for the sake of a "niche"?

If I must be honest with you, niched authors are the most successful. Point. Blank. Period. As stated, Rowling writes under a second pen name. I write under a second pen name. By no means am I telling you to limit yourself. Write what you want to write. Be as diverse as your heart should desire, but I think it is imperative to separate the two.

Become the go-to author for something and you'll ALWAYS have readers who flock to you because of this certain something. As well, some genres and niches run within each other in the writing realm, so you can get away with diversity to a certain extent.

Examples:

Urban + Romance – You can write Urban Romance or either and your audience won't blow up because they are relatively the same, but different in lots of ways. Yet, most authors who write Urban actually have more Romance in their stories than one would think. So, erasing the grit to add a bit more love won't scare away readers so easily.

Romance + Suspense – You can write Romantic Suspense and your readers will possibly dig it.

Christian Fiction + Romance – You can definitely combine the two and write Christian Romance. They'll more than likely go well together. I've seen this task tackled myself.

Paranormal + Urban – Urban Paranormal is what I call it. Many urban authors are dabbling into this field and it is going well for them because they are sticking to the urban genre and incorporating paranormal activity. It is unique, if you ask me.

Now, should you decide to step outside of the entire fence, then you should consider a second pen name. If you're the go-to for a certain type of book and you begin writing randomness for the sake of it, then you begin to confuse your readers. The last thing you want to do is cause confusion, because they fall off like leaves in the dead of the fall if you do. Many people lose readers attempting to genre swap or switch it up in general. I've rarely seen this work well.

Should you desire to write outside of your normal – which we all desire at times – consult with another writer or even your readers. Question what else they'd like to see you write just to test the waters. If the response isn't as strong as you'd like, don't ditch the idea. Simply consider a new pen name where you'll have more freedom.

My second pen name gives me the freedom that Mercy lacks. My readers know me for writing good ass Urban love stories and that is what they expect. The minute I attempted switching up, some went missing. I rectified the situation and created an entirely new persona all together.

Honestly, imagine *Target* opening a car dealership in their parking lot. I honestly think that people would pass the dealership to get inside for the things *Target* are best known for, right? It is kind of the same thing, here.

Imagine *Chick-Fil-A* opening an oil change shop on their lot. I'd be worried about my food and just how sanitary the environment is. If they're going to open a spot like that then they'll possibly choose a different location and name. Imagine *Chick-Fil-A* being at the top of an oil changing sign.

Remember when *IHOP* did the publicity stunt to promote their new burgers? That didn't go over so well. The *International House of Pancakes* announced that they were changing to the *International House of Burgers* and the crowd went BOOOOOOOOO! If you're niched and are doing well, then there is no sense in screwing it up.

Be the person people seek for a certain thing. Don't try to be the Jill of all trades here. It won't end well. This is factual.

➢ How can I become a good storyteller in order to brand within my stories?

Well. I have a few tips.

I tell people all the time, you can either be a great writer or a great storyteller, but if you are both a great writer and great storyteller, then you have a gift that cannot be tamed. I encourage you to use it. If you don't use it, you're doing a disservice to yourself and others like me who loves to read.

I'm not going to talk about being a great writer, but I do want to talk about being a great storyteller. Being a great storyteller means being able to deliver a story in a way that is whimsical, amazing, irresistible, and forces your audience to bow at your feet, metaphorically. I love a good story. People love good stories.

Stories that they can relate to are the best kinds. I tell people all the time that you can brand yourself through writing. You should not just brand yourself through visuals, but you should also brand yourself through the pages of your books because that's when you and the readers are supposed to connect the most.

The way to better connect with your readers is to study your readers; find out what they're having trouble with, what they're going through, what obstacles they are trying to overcome.

Dissect them, study them, know who your audience is and what they have going on in their personal lives.

Once you do this, you can perhaps create stories relating your fictional situations, circumstances and characters to your readers. It's always going to hit home with somebody.

The minute it hits home with someone, you have yourself a lifelong supporter. You are their great escape even for the few hours that they have your book in their hand. That's what you want to be. You want to be someone's great escape.

➤ How do I keep readers intrigued?

One of the things that you can do to keep readers intrigued is to prolong the cheer. When I say prolong the cheer, I mean to extend that scene that's going to make them clap or cry. Prolong that good ending. I don't mean drag your story out. Just don't give them what they want immediately, because then the interest may not be there.

What you want to do to assure you retain their interest is to make sure your journey to that moment that incites clapping – or crying – is highly adventurous. It should continuously get better and better as it leads up to whatever is the major key event.

Let's say a couple completely opposite of one another are fighting to get their way to each other, you don't just bring them together during the middle of the book. You save that for about three-fourths of the book or the very end.

Basically, you don't want to solve the problem you presented too soon. The problem is the reason why you are writing the book, it shouldn't be resolved immediately.

Before you solve that problem, you want to make sure to take them on a great adventure. Don't just give them that happy ending they expect. Prolong the solutions and galvanize your audience.

Another way is to go beneath the surface. Do not be an on the surface, black and white writer. Give compelling details. Tap into who your characters really are. This ties back to character development. You want to make sure that your readers are familiar with your characters while you're writing. You don't want to leave anything to question when it comes to your characters and, subsequently, your storytelling.

You want to make sure that you are very clear and you've gained the clarity of your targeted readers. Don't just tell me about an event, describe the event; how it happened, when it happened, where it happened, why it happened. Make me feel like I'm part of the story.

When you go in depth, it makes you connect with your readers on a deeper level because you begin to stir up emotions. Anytime you can stir a reader's emotions, nine times out of ten, you got them hooked whether they're upset or whether they're happy.

If they're angry, they're going to try to read until they get happy. If they're happy, they're just going to spread the word and bring you in more readers. Either way, you win.

The protagonist is the good guy. The antagonist is the villain. I'm going to tell you one way to capture your audience's attention and keep it. One way to win your audience over is to improve the antagonist.

Turn the enemy into a protagonist and I guarantee you, they'll love you forever because they'll have mixed feelings. To see that revolution is eye-opening for readers. This is because they haven't done all good their whole life. Right?
For them to know that the bad guy can be a good guy, it's like a breath of fresh air for them. You never know what they're doing, or what they're going through, or what they've done to get where they are. When you flip that, it's amazing to see. As a reader, I've experienced it, and it's amazing.

TAKEAWAYS

_____

_____

_____

_____

_____

_____

_____

_____

_____

_____

_____

_____

_____

_____

_____

_____

_____

_____

_____

TAKEAWAYS

_____

_____

_____

_____

_____

_____

_____

_____

_____

_____

_____

_____

_____

_____

_____

_____

_____

_____

Chapter Four

Branding with $0

Three years ago, when I published my first book, I was dead broke. I mean, so broke I was on a Pay As You Go T-Mobile plan. I would pay my bills and at the end of the month, hope that I had money to put money on my phone. I was extremely broke. I was living in a situation that I didn't want to live in just to keep myself from going under water. I was in a deep depression that I didn't even know I was in until I came out.

When I started my brand and when I started my business, I had zero dollars. I didn't have any money besides my bill money. I was able to build a brand with longevity just by being visible and navigating my way through the industry with zero dollars. I knew how to open my mouth and know how to get in front of the people that I needed to be in front of. I've been through this myself, I know what works and what was a fail. So, I am going to teach you how to do the same.

Be visible

Always showing up is important. Whether you are showing up ill-prepared or you show up not knowing, the fact that you showed up speaks volumes. It means that you are at least trying. If you show up and don't know anything or don't have anything, be completely honest.

Listen, we identify more with people who are not perfect. Perfection is a problem in the industry. We want to show you the glitz and the glam, we never want to show the behind the scenes. So be very truthful with yourself. Show up. Just, show up. You cannot afford not to show up. With that said, I am always there. I am always in your face.

The reason I am in your face is that I have something to say and I want you to listen. I have something to share with you. If I'm not there in your face, how can I do that? I don't need you to come find me. If people don't know who you are, you have to put yourself in front of them and tell them who you are. They won't know who you are to search your name. They won't know who you are to come looking for you.

You have to continue to remain visible. Put yourself in their face. Make sure that you are always showing up. I did a visibility challenge in November and December for my business. Within that two months, I made so many new connections. I banked so much money and gained many new clients. No, I did not have it all together all the time, but I showed up.

It is all about perception. It is about how you want to be perceived, it is how you should show up. Perception is power. The amount of perception that you have over them, the more power you have over them. So, show up in the manner that you want them to perceive. If you want to become visible in a positively notable manner, be a man of your word. What you say you do, you do.

If I say I am going to do something, I am going to do it. If I tell my clients I am going to do something, it gets done, unless life happens. Life will happen, and you can't stop life from happening.

However, if you build the perception that you get it done, they'd trust that as soon as you can, it'll be done. Visibility cost no money. Post on IG every day. Post about what you are doing. Use IG stories. If you are writing, let them see that you are writing. If you are working with a client, let them see that you are doing that. As long as you are valuable, you will always have a seat at the table. If you prove yourself valuable, they will always have room for you. Plus, they'll always have your back.

Be Valuable

My suggestion to you is to not jump out the window and start servicing people. My value came from my books. I was my very own testimony. I had over thirty-five books out. People thought that if I had so many books out, then I could help them with their books. That is how my business got started. It spoke for itself. If you have no testimonies yet, you need to have something to bring to the table when you are visible.

You want to make sure you have something to bring to the table. Make sure that you are not just posting cute photos on *IG*. Make sure that you are getting to the nitty gritty about your business. Show them how you can help with your services. How can you be of value to them? Make sure that you are hitting pain points. Let them know that you are their sweet point. Here is your pain point and here is where I can help you. Let them know how you can help, and then actually help them.

It takes so much practice to be great. While you are practicing, be of value. Service people for free. I serviced people for free for a long time before I started charging for my services. Don't think that you are being some type of sourpuss for giving someone something for free. At the beginning, that may be needed. That is the truth. That is how you get to practice. That is how you get testimonies. That is how you find out exactly what you are doing and what services you can provide.

Be valuable. Give valuable content. Give valuable information. Give things your audience may want to know but don't know already. Make sure you are giving them helpful information. Especially if it does not hurt your business. Especially if it does not clash with the services that you are offering. Basically, give some resources, but don't give them all your secrets.

For example, I am a publisher so I won't give them my top-secret methods to publishing my books, but I do provide resources to help them learn. Sometimes, you have things that you just don't give away but give them little bits and pieces of information. When you give them value, they know that you are the source. They will keep coming to you because they want to learn more and more. That is how you build your clients. That is how you build bank.

Entrepreneurship is a give-and-take situation. Many entrepreneurs want to come and just take, take, take and don't provide any VALUE. That is where they mess up. If you give them a little bit, they give you a little more. You give something to them, they give something to you. You don't want to just take their money, and not offer them anything. You have to give them some type of value. *Target* will take my money, but I know the value and quality is worth it.

Content

You can deliver tons of content and advertisement for zero dollars. I have the deets on the websites to make all of these possible. Content is

Facebook, *Instagram*, email list, your *Snapchat*, *Twitter*, *Periscope*. Any social media platform can be your content space. The internet is a blessing to entrepreneurs.

People are building million-dollar businesses strictly from the internet, and you can do the same thing. Plus, you can do it starting at zero dollars. Millionaires weren't always millionaires. Billionaires weren't always billionaires. They had to start somewhere. A lot of them started with zero dollars. Everything in this chapter is free.

You want to give very strong and powerful content. It should be content that reflects you and the manner that you want to be perceived as. You want it to speak to who you are as a person and who you are as a brand. Make sure the content is meaningful. You don't want to be giving stank, rusty and dusty content.

For instance, I want to be the cutesy, know-it-all author. People automatically think the girl with glasses, with her hair in a ponytail, and her back slouched. I want them to know that authors aren't always those type of people. We are fashionable and we are cute. We keep our hair done. I wanted to reverse the thought of what being an author actually is because they put us into this category and it is not true. I also want to be the go-to person for all things literary.

I offer value to my audience. I may put up a cute selfie. I will record a hair tutorial. I will say "Hey, I made this wig in forty-five minutes and I will show you how to do it." They've categorized us, stereotyped us, and I am breaking those stereotypes. I am breaking all those boundaries that have been set. I am also the person for those people who thought they wanted to be an author for so long but couldn't do it.

I am letting them know that I am pushing these boundaries and stepping on these parameters and passing them. I'm surpassing greatness, and I am very inspirational. I am very transparent. I don't hold anything back. I come off as that way. I have nothing to hide from anyone. I feel like whoever I am, or whatever I am, God made me this person, and if you can't accept me for who I am, screw you.

That is what my content shows. It reflects Mercy B Carruthers and no one else. I cannot make this stuff up. I cannot mimic this stuff from anyone else. I have to produce content that is directly about the perception that I want when people think of me. This is free. It doesn't take anything to take a selfie and post it to your *Instagram*. Then give them a caption that is related to books, your life or inspiration. Content is very important.

This goes back to the value and visibility. Make sure your content is valuable. Make sure that your content matters. If it only matters to you, that won't help. You are not selling to yourself. You are not self-satisfying. What you're doing is trying to capture your audience. So, make sure your content goes well with your audience.

Make Connections

Another thing you want to do while you don't have money is make connections. You need to make connections with people that you can bring value to and they can bring value to you. A good connection is not you being connected with someone else who is very well-connected in your industry.

A great connection is when you find someone that can offer you value and you can do the same thing in return. Don't try to go connect with people because he or she has the juice. You need to be able to pour some juice into their cup as well. Don't try to ride anyone's coattail. What you will want to do is make sure that you are bringing value to someone else because they will spread the word. If you help them in any way, the word is going to spread. So, make the connection while you don't have the money.

Ways to make a connection with an author is liking an author's post. Sharing their releases. Jump into their DMs and congratulating them on an accomplishment. I send emails to other business women that I see doing their thing. I like to send "I see you" emails. I simply say "Hey girl, I see you. I see you getting down. You are killing it girl." Sometimes people need to see and hear that.

Even if it is just a simple email that says I see you, I've seen you and I love what you are doing. That is a connection that has been made. Even though you haven't done anything for you, it can start there. It means I like what you are doing. People remember that. SO, now when they see you on *Instagram*, *Facebook* or even in public, they see you now.

All these things lay a foundation for your business when you get the money. The misconceptions come when you think you need a lot of money to start your business. Having no money does not mean that you cannot start. It is not always about money. It takes more time researching and gaining knowledge than it does funds to start a business. It cost more time, resources and knowledge than it does funds in order to keep that business afloat. All of those resources are not paid resources.

Here is an example. Many celebrities start so many overnight businesses. Why? Because they have the money. They start the business, and then in a couple of months to a year, the business is dissolved. They've stopped it. You never hear anything else about it. You want to know why? They had the funds, but they didn't have the resources or knowledge.

They didn't lay a foundation. They had the funds, but they didn't have a foundation. If you start with a great foundation, you should be good. You can continue to build on that solid foundation. They only had the money part, but none of the other essential keys to start and keep a business.

FREE RESOURCES TO START

EMAIL PROVIDER: *MailChimp* **or** *Constant Contact*

Email lists are very important when it comes to managing your business. You can manage your clients, potential customers and gain repeat customers. Be sure to get yourself a list started on *MailChimp.com* because it is completely free. You just follow the quick and easy prompts and your list is ready to grow.

Anytime you are ready to send out emails. Anytime you are ready to begin promotions. Whenever you drop a new product or service. It is great for when you are ready to finally launch your business. You will have the emails there, so you are not launching to ghosts. You can embed the code on your website, or you can simply drop the code on your social media accounts and start collecting emails.

WEBSITE PROVIDER: *Wix*

Wix.com is a website to create free websites. I personally use *Squarespace*, which is twenty-five dollars per month. If you don't have twenty-five dollars to spare a month right now, you can use *Wix.com* and get a free website. You can buy a domain from *GoDaddy* for about twelve dollars. They run tons of sales, and some are six dollars, five dollars or even ninety-nine cents. This is not necessary because *Wix* will provide a free domain for you. If you decide to link your personal domain to *Wix*, they will charge you for that.

CONTENT CREATION: PicMonkey.com or Canva.com

If you want to create graphics for your website, *Instagram*, *Facebook* or any other reason, these two sites are completely free. They both offer paid accounts, but they are not necessary to make graphics. Do not purchase the paid versions unless your business needs grow.

You can even create yourself a temporary logo on both of these sites to begin. You don't need to have tons of graphic design experience to create your logo. *Canva* even has templates where you change words and colors to fit your brand. When starting out, it is pointless to worry about having this beautiful brand and having no value to add to it. A logo will not make your business, your business will make the logo. People won't even notice how good or bad your logo is if you are the best at what you are doing.

FREE ADVERTISEMENT: EVERY SOCIAL MEDIA PLATFORM

Facebook, LinkedIn, Instagram. Any place that allows you to post for free, utilize it. Post your links. Connect with people. Starting a business is not about the money. You can get your business started with no money in your pocket. It is possible. I struggled in the being stages, and I had zero dollars to spare. I did everything for free until I started making money.

PHOTOGRAPHY: YOUR PHONE

You can get away with taking a professional and quality picture with your smartphone. All you need is a tripod and your phone. Go outside and have a shoot. Sunlight is the best lighting, so you will not need to purchase lighting. You don't necessarily need the tripod. Prop it up on something, turn on the self-timer and get into position.

TAKEAWAYS

TAKEAWAYS

_____

_____

_____

_____

_____

_____

_____

_____

_____

_____

_____

_____

_____

_____

_____

_____

_____

_____

_____

Chapter Five

Setting Your Brand on Autopilot

Email automation is a service that your email provider offers with paid and/or free versions. Sometimes free plans have email automation too. This feature helps you schedule emails ahead of time to be sent to your designated list. When planning your monthly content, automation is a key component. Rather than getting flustered trying to rush out emails, with automation you're covered.

Ways to use automation.

You can use automation to send out sneak peeks, announce giveaways, deliver important messages, and keep readers informed. It is also great for dropping book links on release day, give thanks for readers who supported your release and gift prizes for contests.

➢ How to automate?

Starting the automation is super simple. Your email provider offers templates where you can plug in your content, images and brand colors. Once you have the newsletter set up the way you desire, instead of clicking send, you click schedule. On the scheduling page, you choose what day and time to send out your emails.

➢ Why automate?

When you are creating your book campaign for your release, you should have a pre-release email sequence. You should also have a post-release sequence.

An automated book campaign should consist of at least three emails. A pre-release email should announce the upcoming release of your book. This email should have your book title, cover, and the synopsis.

You can give a timeframe for the release date or give the actual release date if you already have it. This email should not include any links unless you are linking them to your website for a sneak peek or blog post related to the book.

On your release day, you should announce that your book is now available and post the links to purchase. You may share a sneak peek or a tidbit of information about the book to make them want to click the link you provided.

A post-release email will thank everyone for supporting your release and remind those who haven't purchased your new release that it is available. This email should also include the link to purchase. Providing your links makes it easy for your readers to 1-Click the releases.

Always include a graphic in your emails. Whether it be your book cover, a picture of you or a character visual. You can even design cute litter graphics for emails. Be sure to also have catchy and engaging subject lines, so your readers want to open your emails and click your links.

Welcome email sequence.

An email list is a way to directly contact people who've gravitated to you and your books. With an email list, you are connecting with people who are genuinely interested in you, rather than blind link dropping. Blind link dropping is putting your book link in various groups and hoping someone buys your book.

The people in those groups most likely don't know. They won't be interested in you. Plus, they see a million authors dropping their links in those groups, so you're just one in a million. Your list is specific to your personal audience. People who expressed their interest in your literary endeavors at some point and time.

Ways to build your list.

Free content is a good way to help build a list. Provide an incentive. You can offer the first three chapters of your next release or an exclusive sneak peek for signing up.

For example, I talked about building influence and getting readers in your corner. So, you may send out a post on social media that says something like, "I'm about to share a free story, sign up for my email list to receive it straight to your inbox." This exposes them to your writing, and they know if you are any good or not.

Readers are leery of just buying anybody's books anymore because writing has become so easy that some authors do not put time or effort into the crat. They release garbage and pass it off as a book. Readers avoid this, so getting them on your lists and showing them what you can do is a surefire way to gain a new reader.

Another way to gain new readers is by posting on your accounts. "Sneak peek going out tonight! Sign up for my email list to get a taste of my upcoming release," then drop the link so they can easily sign up. All of the posts about your book that you usually post to your business page, you can now send to your individualized email list.

Even if you just grab two or three emails a day, that's sixty to ninety emails by the month's end. Email capturing is not easy, so what you have to do is give them something, and you got to take something. What you're taking is their email and their interest. Now you have to keep in contact with them.

Take *Forever 21* for instance, whenever you go to their website, you see a lightbox drop down that says. "Ten percent off by signing up for our newsletter." Any online store you visit they are offering some type of discount or freebie in return for your email address. They want you on their list.

They want to keep in constant contact with you because you are interested in them. You came on their site, so you have to care about their products. Once they capture your email. They are sending you sales pitches. Every day I get an email from *Forever 21*. I get one from *Saks Fifth Avenue*, *Gucci* and everywhere else I shop online because I opted for their newsletter when I went on their site to buy something. Now, I find myself buying something because when I open those emails, I wind up on their site. Why? Because they stayed in my face. The influenced my decision with their constant contact and presence.

You don't have to send emails as often as those stores, but make sure you are there enough, so they don't forget you. Pop in and drop links to remind them to catch up on a series because you started working on the next installment. Let them know you started working on a new story and it may be released within the next thirty days. You can reach out in any way you want, just reach out to them via your email list.

TAKEAWAYS

_____

_____

_____

_____

_____

_____

_____

_____

_____

_____

_____

_____

_____

_____

_____

_____

_____

_____

_____

TAKEAWAYS

Chapter Six

Building a Standout Brand in a Saturated Market

*This industry is so **saturated**.*

I hear it so much that it makes my ears burn. So. No industry is too saturated for your presence. Frankly, if you're busy focusing on saturation then you're coming in with the wrong attitude. Worry about yourself and how you can rise above the saturation that you have no reason being concerned about.

The beauty industry is 'saturated' but do you think that stopped Rihanna?

The rap industry is 'saturated' but do you think that stopped Drake or J. Cole?

The writing industry is 'saturated' (y'all words, not mine), but do you think that stopped Mercy B?

The film industry is 'saturated' but do you think that stopped Denzel?

The music industry is "saturated" but do you think that stopped Beyoncé?

A saturated industry is no excuse for you to sit in a puddle of tears and pout because you're not standing out amongst others.

Ask yourself:

- Are you really doing what it takes to rise above and become notable?
- What is it about you that should make readers flock at your presence?
- How are you different from the others?
- How are you showing readers that you are different from others?
- What makes you special? (Everyone is special in their own right.)
- Why should readers choose you?

➢ How do I stand out?

Branding. Hang on to every piece of advice that has been shared in this book and use it to the best of your ability. Don't shy away from the challenge. Embrace it. While up to this point, I've shared the intangible when it comes to branding – which is most important. There is a portion where I'll share the physical nature of branding in which you should try your best to master.

In order to standout, you must:

- **Be confident**.
  People can smell fear from a mile away. Don't be timid. Find the confidence you lack and show up every day with this confidence.

- **Know your product**.
  Study your product as if it isn't something you produced. Know what you're writing, why you're writing it, and who it may appeal. Know it inside and out.

- **Put trust in your product**.
  If you don't trust your product, why should others? Work on yourself and your product until you're completely satisfied. Don't ever let anything or anyone convince you to rush through your writings. Take your time and produce a product that you can stand behind.

- **Honor your craft and yourself**.

Writers are privileged. I don't care what anyone says. We are. We were built specially and I think we should all understand that. Writing happens to be a weakness of so many people, yet stories are flowing daily for us. We are privileged. Honor that notion and don't ever let anyone cause you to think differently about yourself or your craft.

- **<u>Define yourself often until people know who you are without asking</u>**. Reiterate who you are through your social media, your books, your branding, your methods of communication, and in any other way that you can. Continue to pinpoint the person you are until you no longer have to define yourself and others get the overall ideal of who you are.

- **Reach out to people**. This was an important part of my own elevation in the industry. I wasn't afraid to reach out to the readers that I knew read my books, even if it was only to tell them that I appreciate the support. In return, I made connections and have gained life-long supporters.

- **<u>Support other authors openly</u>**.
Your light won't stop shining because
you are rooting for another author.
Please don't neglect to support
SOMEONE. Because, I'm positive
that there is someone supporting you.
Even if you pick and choose who you
support, support them fully. When
they see this, they'll return the favor
and you will be placed in front of their
audience as well, which may
accompany readers that you wouldn't
have been able to reach had they not
shared your links or mentioned your
name.

- **<u>Be genuine</u>**.
This is self-explanatory. Being anyone
but yourself is exhausting and I highly
suggest that you don't try it. The
people who are for you will find you.
Don't ever become someone you're
not, because you'll never be able to be
yourself again. At least not when it
really matters.

- **Create a safe space for your readers**.

Readers just want to be their little *sophistaratchet* selves and you should let them. Some are married and don't want to lust over fictional characters on their main page because their husbands are always on go mode (lol). Some are heavily involved in the church and don't want pastor knowing what they do on their free time. Give your readers a place to let loose and be who they are dying to be on the inside, a fan of your work. You should see the unearthing that happens in reader groups. It is amazing and the funniest thing ever. Don't let your readers keep this goodness to themselves. Gather them with other people to act a complete fool together. They'll love you for life if you do.

- **Spend at least thirty minutes each day dedicated to bettering your brand**.
  Each day or every other day, discover ways to enhance your brand or better yourself as a writer. Even if it is reading a chapter from a literary help book to improve your craft. Do it. If it is spending a half hour creating

graphics for your upcoming release. Do it. If it is improving the cover you made the day before to better appeal to your audience. Do it.

- **<u>Educate yourself</u>.**
  Don't ever get to the point where you think that you can't learn anything from anyone. Remain a student. Study your craft. Billionaires are avid readers, understanding that they must continue to educate themselves and continue to be well versed. What makes you any different? There are tons of books based on writing and perfecting your craft. Buy them and study them from the front page to the back. Also, read outside of your genre. Don't limit yourself or your capabilities.

- **Always find new ways to communicate with your audience**.
  Speak their language and when they decide to change the dialogue, find out how and why. Don't ever stop communicating with the people who are responsible for your career height and success.

- **Study your audience often**.
  What are they doing? Why are they
  doing it? What are they listening to
  nowadays? What gets them pumped,
  now? Who are they into? What stirs
  them? What leaves them quiet? What
  do they gravitate to the most? Ask
  these questions. It's important that you
  know who is loving on you and why,
  so that you can do more of the stuff
  that makes them love you.

- **Be willing to pivot at any giving
  moment**.
  Never fear the possibility of change.
  Get ready for it and stay ready for it. A
  smart business owner/brand is never
  opposed to pivoting, knowing it is
  required to maintain. When it is time
  to move – move. When it is time to
  stay still – rest.

- **<u>Produce quality work</u>**.
  Self-explanatory. Give them the best
  you've got. Take your time and don't
  rush the process. Continue to prove to
  your readers that you are the golden

one and every time you release a book, they can expect the same thing.

- **Be persistent and consistent**. Deliver with intent. Be purposeful in your writing and delivery. Then, continue to deliver over and over, again.

➢ Others are doing the same thing as I am, so what makes me different?

I don't know what makes you different, but you do. And, if there happens to be nothing that makes you different, then you will never stand out. Here is how you can create the difference.

Do your research. What makes everyone the same? Once you figure this out, find a way to create storylines that are much different. For instance, late last year, I was tired of the entire urban scene and decided to take a stab at some throwback urban. The 'new' urban was draining and hardly made any sense to me, so I found myself searching through the pages of the old classics I read to find solace. I remembered the feeling it gave me and wanted to feel that and help my readers feel that as well.

So, I wrote a series based in the nineties, which my readers happened to love. It was void of the usual violence, killing, saturation of drugs and many other elements that urban is filled with. Yes, these elements were included, but the basis of this story was built around family and the love black families share for one another.

Urban Tales is the name of the series and I still love it to this day. So, as I did, find out how you can implement something different within your writing that will make you stand out from the others. Retracing my words, visit *Branding Through Your Books*, which is only a few chapters above, to learn how to build your brand based on the content you write.

How do I get readers to take a chance on me?

Frankly, take a chance on yourself.

Ask.
Don't be afraid to make a post asking readers to support your book. Don't be afraid to get in their inbox and ask if they will buy your book. When it comes to authors, don't hesitate to ask for the support that you want. Connect with them socially and find out how you can support one another.

Show rather than tell.

If no one cares to hear what you're saying, show them what you mean. Some authors have grown their base by staying quiet and working their asses off. Again, seven forms of contact before the investment. If it is your seventh project and you've been going nonstop. Trust me. People that didn't see you at first, will see you now. Keep in mind, this can only happen with consistency and quality. If you're all over the place, they can see you twenty times and still may not feel the need to invest. Buckle down and brand yourself in a way that they can't turn away if they wanted to,

Stay in their faces.

Be social. If you're new or if you're trying to get more readers, then you have to scout (in some cases, such as the impatient). Find readers – it isn't hard to locate them – and stay on their trail. Friend them. Comment on their posts. Like their pictures. Interact. Genuinely show interest in them and they will return the favor.

Some of my readers are FINE and I make sure that I'm reminding them in case no one else is. Biggin' my readers up happen to be a joy of mine. I also like to joke around with them. This thickens our bond and gives us something to look forward to when we're online at the same time.

Word of mouth.

The best form of promotion (and branding). But, you have to make sure that what is being said about you is GOOD! Of course, not everyone is going to think highly of you or your work. Sometimes, the negative talk still gets the listener to check you out for themselves, which is good. But, we're talking about building a brand here, so it is important that good news is shared about you.

There is nothing like someone else singing your praises. We can say that our work is worthy of one's time, energy and money until we are blue in the face. Yet, the minute someone else says it, there's a switch that flicks on in someone's head and they're suddenly interested.

Think about how the judicial system is set up. Most cases see their day in court (or not) strictly based on the fact that they have a key witness. The offender, or the victim, can give their account of what happened, but it is the key witness' testimony that solidifies the case. Most times, without one, cases crumble from the core. Some cases are even thrown out if the witness recants their statement or decides against testifying altogether.

Well, the same concept pertains to your readers and the word of mouth. The testimony of your readers will outweigh yours any day. They are your witnesses that your content is badass. Let them sing your praises and tell others about you.

This is called delegation. It is tried and true when it comes to gaining new readers. Current readers are the best way to gain new readers. They will go out and grab them for you. Your only job is to deliver them quality work that they can boast about. Give them a reason to brag.

Be so good they can't ignore you.

Be so good that they can't help but to stop and try you out! All they need is a sample and they're hooked.

TAKEAWAYS

_____

_____

_____

_____

_____

_____

_____

_____

_____

_____

_____

_____

_____

_____

_____

_____

_____

_____

TAKEAWAYS

Part Two

Elements of Branding

Choosing a name for your brand.

This happens to be the simplest aspect of branding that authors tend to master. Choosing a name. Most authors write under their actual name while others chose to write under a pen name. Whichever you choose, make sure you're able to grow with the name and never have to worry about outgrowing the name.

When choosing your author name, try to make sure it is not too complicated so that readers are able to find you with ease. As well, be sure that no one else has the same name so that you all aren't ever confused for one another. Lastly, choose a name that you can live with and live up to.

Potential names:

_____

_____

_____

Choosing your brand's colors.

Choosing your brand colors can be both fun and intimidating. You want to go with colors that are fun and pretty. Truthfully, you should stick with colors that are meaningful. Studies show that certain colors garner the attention of an audience much faster than others. I find myself skimming these colors to choose at least one that I feel is a representation of me. You should do the same.

There is also a list of colors that studies show increases sales. Marketers have tested and discovered a huge difference in sale when these colors are within the mix. They all have different meanings, but serve the same purpose – grabbing the attention of others. Here's a list of those colors:

Red
Blue
Pink
Yellow
Green
Purple
Gold
Orange
Brown
Black

Personally, I wouldn't suggest going with more than three colors for your brand, but people often step outside of the box and have more. Let's decide on what colors best describe you and will help you grab the attention of those you're seeking.

Choose the colors you love the most. Then, narrow them down to your brand's colors (3).

Creating a logo.

This is a topic that I am always hesitant to speak on because it is sensitive for most. For authors, I've seen some of the most horrific logos created for the sake of something pretty, when the logo is not a visual representation of the author or their brand. It is important that you not focus too much on the logo and more about what it represents.

My logo is simple. It is my name. Nothing fancy and nothing too off the wall. I chose this route for several reasons. I never found a decent enough logo to suit my brand and because I felt that my brand stood for more than a pen and some sparkles. My brand is known for sophistication and what better way to portray that than a smooth signature logo?

So, when you're ready to have a logo created, don't overdo it. Please. Simple is best. Most times, people outgrow their logo and find themselves getting a new one each year. Keep it cute and keep it simple.

If you're willing to pay the big bucks to have a logo created, then have your way. If you're looking to create your own logo and save yourself some money, it is totally possible. There are websites for you to conduct this task and continue altering your logo until it is perfect.

PicMonkey

LogoGarden
Canva

Logo idea?

Your perception.

Perception is power. Before presenting yourself to the world (if you're currently an author), decide on how you want to be viewed. This is important because it determines how you will move from this point forward. When you pinpoint the way that you want your brand to be identified, everything you do will matter.

The way you post on social media.
How often you post on social media.
What you post on social media.
How often you interact on social media.
How often you release.
How you promote your brand.
The tools you use.
The message you convey.
The image of yourself, your brand and your books.

Think about it. Long and hard. How do you want to be identified?

Explain:

_____

_____

Your Bio.

Bios are important for authors, and for that matter, anyone in business. I've designed websites for many authors and when I request a bio, there aren't many of them that actually have one. Or, I'm sent an extra-long bio that talks about when they were five and fell off of the steps. Blah. Blah. Blah. No one cares about when you fell off the steps at five.

Your bio should be no more than four paragraphs. Let's face it. Readers want to get to the goods. Besides, they have enough reading to do. Don't give them a heap more. Your bio should be short, straight to the point and cute.

Here's my suggestive bio:

First paragraph is your introduction; who you are now, and where you are now.

Second paragraph is a brief glimpse of your history and how it impacted who you are today.

Third paragraph is where you list your accolades and plans of the future.

Fourth paragraph is completely optional.

#1.

#2.

#3.

#4.

Brands you love.

I know you've been watching brands and possibly love the way they've branded themselves. In your head, you want to do the same. I'm here to tell you that you're able. You've possibly been stalking them for a bit. Don't let that energy go to waste.

Now, before we move on, I must tell you that I do not condone COPYING or STEALING from others in no form or fashion.

Moving forward, pay close attention to the things you actually love about this brand. Find out what is so appealing to you and others. Try to think of ways that you can implemented these tactics into your brand without COPYING their work.

For instance, there was one brand in particular that I adored. After following this brand for so long, I realized there wasn't much special about the brand in particular, but the amount of effort and energy this brand put into their visuals set them apart from brands just like them. So, because I understood this, what do you think I did? I began putting more thought and effort into my visuals as well. And, guess what? It worked!

Brands you love and why you love them.

#1.

_____

_____

_____

_____

#2.

_____

_____

_____

_____

#3.

_____

_____

_____

Social Media

Once you've gotten the key elements of your brand in order (perception, logo, colors, and all of that good stuff), then you will need to make sure that your social media reflects the brand module that you have chosen. "Stay on brand," is what many entrepreneurs say.

When on your social media, no one should have to guess who you are or what it is that you do. Within the first five seconds of visiting your page, they should have an idea that you're an author and you write books. It only takes a quick second for them to click off. Don't allow that to happen by posting unnecessary content.

I try to keep personal pictures to a minimum. My daughter is rarely posted on my social media, though I talk about her often. I talk about her because it opens dialogue between the readers that are mothers too. But, I don't clutter my feed with her photos or anything of that nature, because I understand that promoting motherhood isn't a part of my brand. Maybe it will be in the future, but it isn't for now.

Pictures: Avoid posting too much randomness unless you're on your personal social media. If possible, try to post things that reflect who you are as both a writer and a person. On platforms such as *Instagram* – which is all about pictures – be intentional with the pictures you take. Showcase behind the scenes. Let readers know you're working.

Captions: Book related or author related captions always stir readers. Post them as often as possible. Examples are on my *Instagram* page (www.instagram.com/mercybcarruthers).

Ways you wish to clean up your social media:

_____

_____

_____

_____

Ways to improve your social media:

_____

_____

_____

Graphics

Graphics are a plus for literature. Just because you write books does not mean you cannot use graphics. In fact, you should use graphics because it will draw a reader to your words. As I've said before, people naturally gravitate to pictures before they see or read words. So, the best way to combat this is to put the words on a picture. Dress it up and make it real for them.

Graphics are needed for your book campaign. They're needed for your email newsletters because you need some things to just pop out at them. You need some things to keep their attention.

Our attention span, as humans, is short, so by seeing pretty, colorful words and pictures, we stay engaged. Don't go putting selfies on your graphics for your website. They can go on your social media, occasionally, but again, you want professional-quality graphics.

You have to remember you are an entrepreneur. You are building a brand. Even as an author, you are a brand. Your books are an extension of your brand. So, you need to make sure you look the part online. You need graphics that exemplify your stance and how you want to be perceived. Like I talked about before, your graphics are important for building your brand.

You have to tell yourself that you are trying to create a name for yourself and in order for you to get the audience that you desire, you need to look the part. Looking the part helps build your social presence and following. This, in turn, builds your influence and naturally, your bank account.

You can create graphics with shareable quotes that link back to you. You do this by putting a watermark on your images. The watermark can be your logo, your social handles, or a personal hashtag that you are trying to populate for yourself.

These quotes should be ones that you know everyone can relate to. They need to be easy to repost without having to crop or alter. Taking your creation of graphics seriously can elevate your reach on social media.

This means that no matter who puts it up, they know it came from you. For instance, I have a post I created with some Amber Rose emoji pack graphics and it went viral. Celebrities were sharing the post, and it didn't matter because people knew it came from me. My name was on it, and it drove a large amount of traffic to my *Instagram* account. Once the traffic makes it back to your social media page, you don't want it to be a mess. You want a cohesive and curated page.

You want people to look at the first few posts on your page at any given time and know exactly who you are and what you stand for. Your graphics will do this for you. When you have pretty graphics, colorful quotes and post, they can retweet or repost, they are more likely to remain engaged with you.

They are more inclined to hit the follow button. They are more inclined to get on your list and want to interact with you. People see your brand before they see your books or even reach out to you, so make them want to get to know you and your work.

Graphics are also important because you can use graphics to spice up your regular pictures. You can spice up your website. Your graphics spice up your newsletters, announcements and giveaways. Planning your content calendar makes creating graphics easier.

You know exactly what types of posts you need to create and when they will be posted. You know the color schemes, what you are promoting and what fonts will go over well with the content for that promotion. This helps you batch process your graphics.

Everybody always says "Hey, Mercy, I love your social media. How do you do these things? How do you get your social media to look the way it is? It just looks so put together. You can do the same thing. Making excessive graphics is a waste of time. It is not necessary. I want you to make graphics that are helpful to your brand.

Don't go design crazy. Don't get hung up on graphic designing and forget the purpose of having the graphics. Remember you want to post with a purpose when building your brand. You are going to love creating them but have some restraint because creating pointless graphics will take up a lot of time you could have dedicated to maybe writing your book or researching your target market. Make sure you cover the important graphics first.

Listing your book release ideas before designing helps prevent design overload. If you want to have coming soon on one side and the book cover on the other side, have that on your calendar. If you want to have coming soon on the top, the book cover in the middle, and your name at the bottom, it should be on your list.

You may want to have your logo on one side and your book on the other, add it to your list. You can even have your book on one side and your picture on the other side. Let them know that you're the author. Any other ideas that you have for your book and your release, go ahead and plan it out before you begin designing. This way you can productively batch process these images.

Graphics are also great for your *Facebook* business page. On *Canva*, they have templates that are the exact dimensions that you need for the different social media accounts. This help prevents you from having to crop images and risk losing some of your valuable information on the graphics.

You should have a really engaging and captivating *Facebook* header for your business page, your profile page, and your group. These headers are the first thing that the members or followers will see. It also attracts new members and followers without you having to do anything. Make sure you have your name on it. It should also have your social media handles where you want your readers to engage with you. If you want, you can have a photo of yourself. I suggest a photo of you just to make it more personal.

You also need to make sure that everything is accurate and up-to-date on your *Facebook* business page. If you don't have a *Facebook* business page, you should get one today! In place of the cover header, you can have a bio graphic which has your photo and your bio on opposite sides, I suggest creating a full header, but this can be in place of that while you are designing the header.

These header graphics eliminate the guessing the reader would have to do to find out who you are and what you write.

The last place your graphics will be great use is your *Facebook* group. Make graphics of your writing process. Take a photo from overhead of your hands on the computer keyboard and put some pretty text on top that lets your readers know that you are currently writing. Post cute little phrases on your photos to pull people in and invite them to view your process. Also, make a group cover graphic just like you would for your *Facebook* business page.

You can also make a header graphic for your regular profile page too. This is where all the branding for zero dollars tips come into play. Quality photos for zero dollars are easily attainable with a smartphone camera, tripod and some sunlight. You can have professional photos in minutes, and all you have to do is position your camera, pose and snap the photo.

These photos grab people's attention and increase engagement. The number one thing is to learn how you make yourself a professional. You have to face it. Your bestie may not always take the best photos, so you can prop your camera up somewhere, set the self-timer and pose. The camera does the rest.

Those pictures can be used on social media, on your website, or on your book campaign emails. The possibilities are really endless when you have professional quality photos. You can recreate tons of graphics with a few great photographs. When building a following, you want people to share, repost and retweet your posts.

So, make sure they are of exceptional quality. No one wants to share crappy and grainy photos. No one wants to scroll down a page with tons of horrible photos with glitches and poor lighting. Make sure you are posting share-worthy content. That starts with great graphics and pictures. You want something good enough for people to repost.

You may not know this, but you can get a lot of followers from the discovery page. When you get on a discovery page, you don't want a crappy, furtive photo. You don't want a crappy picture. You don't want a blurry image because the people on the discovery page are going to have clear, pretty pictures. You stand out with great pictures. You don't want to be the one that falls through the cracks because your images are poor quality.

Discovery page images are based on followers and likes. They just randomly choose people to put on a discovery page based on what the person has liked recently or who they follow. It is based on what content that they're always looking at, the videos that they are always playing. The pages they always go to, the types of posts they like on the discovery page. They analyze what you're looking at, and they show you stuff where you'd be more prone to engage. So, you never know when you'll land on someone's discovery page. Always look your best on social media. This requires amazing graphics.

Beautiful photos make people engage. Beautiful photos keep them waiting for more. Beautiful photos make them tell their friends about them. They'll tell them to look at a page, they'll even tag people in your pictures. You want people to get to you. You want to get people buzzing about your posts. That's possible if you have great content. They're going start clicking on your website. Now you have new people, new followers and potential new readers.

Instagram is going to be leading readers to your page. That's because they know that this is your audience. Especially if your *Instagram* is connected to your *Facebook* business page, which I highly recommend. This allows ad campaigns on *Instagram*.

Tools for authors and readers to stay connected.

Author Central

Have you created an account on *Author Central*? If not, then you should. In fact, take a look at my author central. Look me up on *Amazon* under Mercy B. Some authors aren't sure what to include in their AC profile, but here are some elements to implement.

- Brief bio
- Social media handles (you're unable to have clickable links for the time being)
- Website link to be copied and pasted
- Newsletter link to be copied and pasted
- Directions for readers to follow you (click the yellow follow button) so that they can be updated when you release new content. Amazon will keep them informed when your books release.

Goodreads

The same pretty much goes for *Goodreads*. Make sure that all of your books are posted to your account. If not, contact them by sending an email and they are really good about straightening out your catalog. As for your profile, the same elements apply.

- Brief bio
- Social media handles
- Website link
- Newsletter link
- Directions for readers to follow you

Facebook Business Page

Facebook business pages are very useful when utilized properly. Please be advised that *Facebook* business pages are a way for *Facebook* to make money. When you post to these pages, you don't get as much traction unless you pay to promote the post. Most of your audience won't see the posts you put on a business page.

I would create a *Facebook* group because your audience members will possibly be more responsive to a group conversation. They can also feel more confident in posting because not everyone can see it. Your group is where you can be sure people will see your post. *Facebook* even notifies group members when they miss a post, so you don't have to hound people for replies.

Yet, I have witnessed authors ONLY use their *Facebook* business page and come out on the winning end. I use mine often and get a pretty good response. Just recently, I decided to stop giving my coins to *Facebook* and refuse to promote posts on my business page. I have over seven thousand likes on my page and I feel like all seven thousand people should be seeing my posts. However, *Facebook* requires them to like and follow your page to see what you post. It is stupid, but it is how they are making their money.

Website

I love when authors have means of connecting with their readers outside of social media. Websites happen to be my favorite way of connecting. I think every author should have one. A website is a home for your brand. People are able to see what you are doing and what you have to offer.

Your social media changes and you aren't always screaming about what you are doing, your website is your home. Every time they are on your website, they can see what you are doing. You. They won't have to fish around for content. Your website is all things you.

As a professional, as a brand, as an entrepreneur, you should have a website. As an author, you are an entrepreneur. You are your own business, and you should have your own website. You are trying to build your own following. If you want to be your own, you want to look very professional.

Email list for newsletters

Refer to Setting Your Brand on Autopilot.

One professional picture

Unless being the face of your brand isn't a part of your brand, then I highly suggest you take at least one professional or semi-professional picture. This doesn't have to cost hundreds of dollars. You can take your own photo, see *Branding with $0.*

Note

I hope that you have found this book helpful in many ways. It was a privilege to grace your home, your hands, your conversation and your mind. It is my wish that information that you read in this book was both fresh and useful.

Mercy B Carruthers

About the Author

As *Mercy*, I am a bonafide Romance cultivator with over 60 titles under my belt. Between the pages and through the bleeding ink of my pen, I urge to create whimsical stories that depict the truth about black love with relative situations, circumstances, and characters. Mercy is a penman derived from a deeper desire to tell of less complex, circumstantial, stereotyped, and biased stories of black and interracial love. My goal is to highlight the misconception that black love stories can be everything BUT pleasant, joyful, everlasting, and beautiful.

In early **2015**, I debuted my very first title, as a published author. Since, I've gone on to create over 60 pieces, **over 54 of them resulting in bestsellers, and collectively published over 140 books!** I've **MERCILESSLY** built a literary empire by breaking every barrier set before me. My world renowned series, **"RahMeek and Bella: A Philly Love Story,"** made it's first appearance in August 2015, sparking my love for literature in the most whimsical manner.

A perimeter pushier and boundary breaker 5'2 force of literature, I've adopted the pseudonym, *The Literary Heroine*. As an independently published author, I debuted my first title in 2015. Since, I've become a resourceful alliance in the literary industry, brushing shoulders with other world-renowned pen pushers and aiding countless authors with the material and coaching needed to tackle their literary career with confidence.

Awards: Female Author of the Year & Romance Author of the Year

Connect with me, socially:

Facebook.com/mercybhere

Instagram.com/mercybcarruthers

Twitter.com/mercybcarruther

The Art of Branding as an African American Storyteller

Made in the USA
Coppell, TX
09 June 2023

17893283R00069